SHT4U2NO

150 Super Hiking Tips
For You To Know

Paul Kautz

Dedication

For all you hikers I have yet to meet on trail.

Hike On!

Table of Contents

Dedication..iii

Acknowledgments.....................................i

Chapter 1 Hold Up There, Friend.....................1

Chapter 2 How Hard Is It?............................7

Chapter 3 Whoosh Flash Boom!.....................13

Chapter 4 Home Away From Home...............23

Chapter 5 Nighty Night...............................31

Chapter 6 Fear Is Heavy..............................35

Chapter 7 Food Fight..................................43

Chapter 8 H2O..55

Chapter 9 Toiletiquette................................63

Chapter 10 Crushing It................................69

Chapter 11 Thrifty, Not Cheap......................75

Chapter 12 Bite, Scratch, & Itch...................83

Chapter 13 They Went That-a-way................91

Chapter 14 Get Buffed or Bonk.....................97

Chapter 15 Do or Die..................................101

Bonus Appendix: Say What?.........................107

About The Author......................................119

Acknowledgments

Special thanks to my wife and hiking partner, Kelly, for doing so much research in the field with me as well as providing valuable criticism of my writing.

Thanks to Dave Windett for answering an online request for an artist from someone he never met on the other side of the ocean, and then creating wonderful illustrations that brought this book to completion.

Chapter 1
Hold Up There, Friend

You may just want to quickly absorb the dozens of tips ahead of you, but there are a few things you should know first to make reading this book more useful.

Right off the bat, you should be skeptical about every piece of advice you get, from me or anyone. If someone says you absolutely must use a Blarvots brand toothbrush with flexible handle and heavy-duty gum pick or else your teeth will fall out on a long hike, warning alarms should be going off in your head. If I mention any brands, it's just because that's what I use, not because I think you should use them. But, of course, I use them because they do the job.

You should also be asking why advice from me is worth anything. Well, I've been backpacking since the early 1980s. I still have an old pair of waffle stomper hiking boots with red laces! Of course, I never wear them now but they used to be the best footwear available. My hiking goals, attitudes, and skills have evolved along with the sport as equipment and accepted practices have changed.

I have experience in all sorts of outdoor living, from family camping to Boy Scout treks to solo thru-hikes. In the past decade, I've spent hundreds of days and nights hiking and sleeping in countless exotic locations, from frozen Minnesota lakes to sultry Costa Rican jungles.

I freely admit that I'm cheap and I'd rather fix something or make something myself than buy something new. This includes making my own gear and re-purposing worn out items for a new use. As a matter of fact, I am still using my first pair of hiking poles that my sons bought for me from Walmart in 2012. They are over 10 years old, the ends are worn down about 2 inches, and I've repaired them twice. But, they still work just fine.

I like to push myself to hike many miles each day on the trail. I want to be safe and comfortable. I enjoy gaining new knowledge and trying new ways to succeed in my endeavors.

I've thru-hiked the Arizona Trail, Ice Age Trail, Pacific Northwest Trail, Superior Hiking Trail, Border Route Trail, Kekekabic Trail, West Coast Trail, and Camino de Costa Rica trail. They range from 50 miles to 1,200 miles. I've hiked solo, with a buddy, and with a group. All of my long hikes have had a few things in common – there are difficult times when I felt like quitting and wonderful times when I couldn't think of any place I'd rather be. I've not been successful on all my long hikes. I stopped once due to injury, and once because I was finding no enjoyment from the hike.

Besides long trails, I've also backpacked for just a week or long weekend many times, but who keeps count of those? Fortunately, the length of a trek doesn't matter much. Skills and knowledge needed for a month are very much the same as those needed for a weekend. Over the hundreds of days and thousands of miles that I've hiked, I've learned and used the tips, habits, and advice ahead of you in this book to stay safe and comfortable, and to succeed most of the time.

As you read these pages, you should consider each tip I offer and decide if it is something you will use or not. That's exactly the sort of decision making you'll need to do when you're out on the trail. Just because someone else does it one way doesn't mean you can't do it another. I'm simply letting you know what works for me in an effort to help you reach a high level of safety, efficiency, and enjoyment quickly.

Be aware of the Say What? appendix at the end of the book. It explains many terms that may be new to you. Things like MYOG, YoYo, and Yogi, for example.

I've tried to make my advice positive and let you know what you *should do* but some things just make more sense by telling you what you *should not do*.

You might want to use a marker to highlight tips you don't want to forget. Folding over the page corner makes finding the good stuff easier, too.

You could carry this book with you on your next hike since it's not very big and doesn't weigh much. Read a tip out loud for your hiking buddy or group and then debate its value as you hike on, or while sitting around camp. I've also heard that reading a couple pages is a great way to help tired hikers fall asleep when nothing else works.

Many of my tips explain *what* to do, but *not how* to do it because there are many possible ways. For example, I believe you should treat drinking water to be safe, but I don't tell you how to treat it because you may prefer a different method than I use.

If you would like more *how* details for any of my tips, I have created a living FAQ page for this book at https://hikingdude.com/sht4u2no.php where you can see what others have asked about or ask your own question.

I sincerely hope this book helps you experience a safe, fun, and successful world of hiking.

Hike On, Dude!

SHT4U2NO

Chapter 2
How Hard Is It?

Long distance hiking is a simple sport. Walk, eat, sleep. Repeat day after day. Even though it's pretty simple, many people who start a long hike fail to finish it. A few guiding ideas will help you succeed on that big trek you are dreaming about.

Tip #1   Start Hiking! It's simple, but the vast majority of people who fail to finish a long hike are the ones who never even take the first step. Someone reads a review of a new book written about a person's hiking adventure, or sees a news story about a long trail, or hears of a friend who hiked for a couple months, or reads a book of hiking tips they got for Christmas, and they get a desire to do a big hike.

After reading a couple more books, or watching a few hours of online hiker videos, many hiker-wannabees figure out that a long hike is a massive project and their dream fades away before it was even attempted. They are too intimidated by the prospects of costs, logistics, and danger to actually make an attempt. But, this isn't you!

Just remember that a long hike is nothing more than a lot of short hikes put together. So, start doing the short hikes to develop good walking muscles and a good walking mindset. This is as simple as walking around your neighborhood for a half hour every morning. Use this time walking to dream about and plan your long hike.

Tip #2   They say the way to eat an elephant is "one bite at a time". Rather than becoming dejected from attempting to plan out one huge 3-month trek, or 1,000 mile hike, I've found it's more manageable to think of a long trek as just a string of week-long backpacking trips. Figuring out the gear, costs, and logistics for a short backpacking outing is much easier. I only need my basic equipment, food for a week, and a map of the trail ahead. There's not much to it.

Once you realize that the next week on trail is just a repeat of this one, and the next repeats that one, week after week, a long hike really does become a sequence of short hikes strung together, with a civilized break between each one in a town along the way to get more food.

Tip #3   Have earned confidence in yourself. A lack of self-confidence prevents many from experiencing a long hike.

I had only a vague idea of what the Arizona Trail would be like as my first long hike, but I was confident in my hiking skills, as well as my camping, cooking, navigating, and safety skills. I was confident because I was experienced from having completed dozens of short backpacking trips in many different environments. I truly believed I would complete the hike as long as I did not get injured too badly. Being confident that you will succeed makes success much more likely.

Tip #4 Gain confidence from competence earned through research, learning, and practice. Some people set off on a long hike as their first backpacking experience, but the success rate is very low for these inexperienced hikers. Learning and preparing in lower stress situations helps build your skills and confidence.

Take a wilderness first aid course to boost your first aid skills. Learn navigation, both with your electronic device as well as with map and compass. Prepare some backpacking meals at home. Go on 2- or 3-day outings to practice your skills with the gear you'll have and in a similar environment as you expect on your longer trek.

Before my first thru-hike, I used all my gear on three separate overnight test hikes. I had set up and taken down camp three times before my trek even started and I had worked out how to use everything I packed. I was never more than a few hours from my car at the trailhead on these practice excursions, in case I had any catastrophic failures. This was training specifically for this long hike, not including the many backpacking trips I had done for years before.

Tip #5   Be flexible. You can be sure that your actual hike will be quite a bit different from your hiking plan that you spent time working out at home. Weather, fatigue, terrain, fellow hikers, and many more surprises will impact your daily progress. You may finish your trek sooner or later than you had planned, but by being willing to go with the flow and modify your itinerary, you will enjoy your hike more and have a higher chance of completing your overall plan.

When hiking the Border Route Trail, through the northern Minnesota wilderness just south of Canada, I had very little idea if the trail tread would be rough, how many blown down trees would barricade it, or how overgrown the brush would be. So, I planned to hike only 8 miles for the first day. I wound up covering 17 miles on a very nice trail before stopping to camp. The next 3 days of trail were extremely rough and I hiked fewer miles, so it all averaged out.

Planning daily miles with an expected finish date weeks away is a sure way to increase stress and reduce enjoyment of a long hike. When the end is a week or less away, it is much easier to set a finish date.

SHT4U2NO

Chapter 3
Whoosh Flash Boom!

When people get injured or killed by weather or other natural occurrences, folks often say there was nothing to be done because it was just "an act of God". Fortunately, there are many things we can do to minimize the risk of those acts happening to us out on the trail.

Tip #6   Keep an eye on the sky. When you stop to enjoy all those great views you hiked so long to reach, take a moment to purposefully observe the sky and air. Has the wind picked up? Has it gotten warmer or cooler? Have clouds become darker, lower, or just more ominous?

Hikers can pass hours trudging along, dutifully navigating the trail ahead of them, while being oblivious to the changing weather. If you notice more wind and cooler temperature, watch the sky more closely for change. If it continues to worsen, ensure you are able to safely continue or start looking for a safe place to camp to wait out the impending storm.

On a trek with Boy Scouts in New Mexico, the wind picked up and the temperature dropped noticeably over a half hour of hiking through forest. Reaching the edge of the forest before a wide open area of a few miles, we could see precipitation falling from large clouds ahead. So, we paused back in the tree cover for about an hour while hail pellets clattered through the branches above us and covered the ground in white. It was much better than being caught out in the open.

Tip #7   Keeping an ear attuned to noises in the sky is important. Thunder, even rumbling off in the distance, should be a warning sign to the tuned in hiker. Estimate how close the lightning is that caused the thunder and monitor it to decide if it is approaching and when you should seek shelter.

Estimating lightning distance is pretty easy, but remember it's only an estimate and wind direction and terrain can limit what you hear. When you see a flash of lightning, start counting seconds. When you hear the thunder, divide the seconds by 5 and that is approximately how many miles away the lightning occurred. Lightning closer than 6 miles is a significant threat and you really should seek shelter. This would be less than 30 seconds from lightning flash to thunder clap. Remain sheltered until 30 minutes after the last lightning flash is seen to give the storm time to pass on by.

The hike up 13,000 foot Cloud Peak in Wyoming, which is above timberline, offers spectacular views. It typically takes about 5 or 6 hours to climb up and 3 or 4 to return, and I've been to the top a handful of times as part of longer backpacking trips. On one hike, about 2/3 of the way up the climb, dark clouds could be seen building many miles to the west but lower than our elevation. We could see that the clouds were definitely moving in our direction, and lightning was silently flashing below them, so the decision was made to abort the summit attempt and retreat down the mountain.

We didn't make it down very far before the clouds blew up the mountainside to meet us. We took shelter from the rain, hail, wind, and lightning by putting on our rain gear and crouching in small pockets between boulders as we spread out in pairs. That was my closest encounter with lightning as the flash of light and crack of thunder were nearly instantaneous.

Tip #8 Shelter from storms out in the wild can be difficult to find. Setting up your tent in a safe place and sitting inside on your sleeping pad is about the best you can do since you will be low and dry. Pick a spot off of ridges, away from individual trees and the tallest trees around, on sandy soil or dry soil, and in a low area but not some place that might flood.

The best natural place to shelter is under a forest canopy. I check out the trees and make sure I don't shelter near a pine tree when I'm in a mostly deciduous forest since pines tend to be very tall and pointy which lightning loves to seek out.

Looking out over the northern Minnesota wilderness from pretty much any vista point on any trail will give a great visual example of this tip. On any far ridge, there is sure to be a red pine or two poking a couple dozen feet above the general birch, poplar, and spruce mixed forest, some with their tops shattered from lightning or broken from high winds.

Tip #9   Know the general weather patterns of the area through which you are hiking. If thunderstorms tend to roll in every afternoon, then plan to be off trail and in camp by that time, or at least taking a sheltered break for a couple hours while the storm passes by.

Tip #10   Know the elevation and exposure of the trail ahead. By reading a topographic map, you can see large, open areas and ridges that you will be crossing. Plan your hike to cross these at safer times of day. At least be more weather vigilant when you approach them and consider taking a rest before crossing them if weather is building.

Tip #11   Check the weather forecast like voting – early and often. Whenever you get phone coverage during your trek, updating the forecast should be one of the first things you do.

If I'm expecting a day of rain in two days, I might cover more miles today and tomorrow since the bad weather will most likely slow me down when it arrives. Or, I might push farther or slow down so I'm in a more protected area when the storm is expected.

Wind can have a big impact on a hike. I was nearly knocked over by the ferocious wind on Kilimanjaro. My shins were covered with pinpricks of blood from sand blown by the desert wind in Arizona. I climbed over or under more than 90 trees from a windstorm in only a 1-mile stretch of the Pacific Northwest Trail.

Tip #12   Weather typically comes from the northwest in most places in North America. If wind is coming from the east or northeast, there's a better chance that foul weather is on the way. Paying constant attention to the environment around you is a good habit to develop in order to be aware of weather changes in time to take action.

Tip #13   When setting up camp, look above you for dead trees and large branches that high winds might knock down. Set your shelter away from them since the wind may pick up during the night.

Wildfire had destroyed the forest along a three mile section of the Pacific Northwest Trail a couple years before I hiked it. With all the standing dead timber, there was no safe place to camp so I pushed farther that day until I exited the burned area before camping.

Tip #14 Wind increases your heat loss by blowing warmed air away from your body. This helps keep hikers cool on hot days, but increases the risk of hypothermia on cooler days. Have an extra clothing layer available as needed as the wind and temperatures change.

Tip #15 Wind also increases evaporation of moisture from your body. Drinking more water on windy days replenishes the lost water. Using lip balm can help prevent dry, cracked lips.

Even on beautiful days of hiking, awareness of the weather is important. A gorgeous, blue sky day still has its potential problems.

Tip #16 Protect yourself from the sun, especially from about 9am until 6pm. Light colored, loose fitting, light weight, long sleeve shirts are best.

Sunscreen on uncovered skin can protect those areas. A common place to forget and get sunburned when wearing short pants is behind the knees. You can gradually reduce cover as your skin tans over the days outdoors, or you can stay covered all the time if the temperature is not too hot.

Since I have no natural head covering, I'm very sensitive to this. Another person hiking with me, who had a full head of hair, had the tops of both his ears covered in blisters from just one morning in the sun with no hat. My nose is the area that I tend to neglect.

Tip #17   A lightweight, inexpensive umbrella is great for sun protection as well as rain protection.

I often took a siesta in the shade for an hour or so around noon on the Arizona Trail to give my skin a break from the most direct sun rays. Sometimes, the only shade was from a saguaro cactus. Sometimes, there was no shade and my umbrella provided it for me.

Tip #18   The sun burns through clouds. Sun protection is always appropriate, even if you can't find the sun in the sky.

Tip #19   Sun glare off water, snow, sand, or light-colored rock can add to sunburn problems, especially your eyeballs. It's always a good idea to wear UV-blocking sunglasses during the day, even cloudy days. Wrap-around glasses, or added side shields help even more.

Chapter 4
Home Away From Home

You will need to find a place to camp every night on the trail. Finding that perfect spot and having the skills to enjoy your time there makes a trek more fun and comfortable, and there is much more to consider than just a picturesque view of the sunset. Hikers will tend to either concentrate their camping in established sites or disperse their camps along a trail that does not have defined sites.

Tip #20   Permanent shelters are a useful hassle. On some popular maintained trails, such as the Appalachian Trail, there are constructed shelters every few miles. These shelters typically have an established toilet, water source, picnic table, and fire ring.

I prefer to avoid camping at permanent shelters because they tend to have rodents, human waste, and heavy traffic. I'll use the toilet there, fill up on water, and make dinner at a picnic table, but then camp farther down the trail where it is cleaner and quieter.

But, hey, using a permanent shelter means you don't need to spend the time to set up your tent which then stays clean and dry for the next day. Plus, you can spend that free time visiting with other hikers and enjoying a community campfire.

Tip #21   Some trails, such as the Superior Hiking Trail, have designated campsites, so plan your day of hiking to ensure you don't run out of daylight far from a designated campsite. Hikers are required to camp at these sites rather than dispersed camping anywhere along the trail.

These campsites are often defined because the trail is passing through private property on an easement. These sites on popular trails also tend to have rodent, waste, and over-use problems, but they simplify the task of deciding where to camp.

Tip #22   An expectation on most trails that have established campsites or shelters is that they are shared by many users. If you set up at a site early, someone else arriving later has a right to find a spot for their tent in the site and stay there as well. This expectation is not universal, so learn the guidelines for the trail you're hiking.

One evening, I arrived at a very popular site on the Superior Hiking Trail where every spot of worn ground was already in use. I had no choice but to set up my tent on the very edge, encroaching on some vegetation and expanding the campsite a bit. I won't complain about the placement of the tents that were already there, but...

Tip #23   If you're first to arrive at a shared camping site, make room for other hikers who may arrive after you. Rather than plopping your tent down in the center, set it up out of the way toward the edge of the site. You'll have a bit quieter spot with less traffic, and there will be room for late arrivals. You both win.

Tip #24   Scope out the terrain of your campsite. Look for dips and swells of the ground to notice where the water will run when it inevitably rains. Position your shelter on a higher spot. Flat is good, a slight slant is better, and ground gradually dropping away on all sides is best for avoiding pooling rainwater.

On an outing in the Boundary Waters Canoe Area Wilderness in Minnesota, we set up a beautiful camp at about noon because a very heavy looking storm was moving towards us from the far horizon. When the storm finally reached us, it rained for over 5 hours and one person's tent completely flooded because it was in a slight dip rather than on a slight rise. This was a matter of a couple inches, so it's an easy thing to miss.

If you are making camp outside of established sites, this is called dispersed camping. It tends to be rougher ground and requires more planning to have a nice night's rest. Since there are no worn tent spots to show where others have camped, all the decision making is up to you. Your main goals should be safety, comfort, and minimizing your impact.

As night was darkening after sunset on the Arizona Trail, we could find no place to camp. The trail cut across the sloping side of a mountain for the next few miles so there were no level areas, and pokey, scratchy plants grew everywhere. We finally just plopped down our pads and sleeping bags right in the trail. It was flat and comfortable, but our planning could have been better.

Tip #25 Low areas such as bottoms of canyons and river valleys tend to get colder at night. Consider making camp a short distance up a hillside to stay warmer.

On the Pacific Northwest Trail, we woke up one chilly morning to frost covering the grass in the small valley where we had camped. Only 50 feet or so in elevation up the hillside, there was no frost and we would have had a warmer night.

Tip #26 Ridges and summits get stronger wind and have higher lightning danger than lower areas. Making camp down the hillside means a safer and quieter night of rest. That sunrise view might be awesome from the top, but you can wake a bit early and hike up there to enjoy it.

After reading the lightning danger signs at trailheads in the Cloud Peak Wilderness of Wyoming for years, I finally asked a wilderness ranger I had met on the trail if anyone had actually been hit by lightning. He knew of two instances – both were tents set up high on rock outcrops with beautiful views of the valleys below.

Tip #27   Camp under a uniform canopy of trees. This provides storm protection, shade, privacy, and better cat hole duff. Camping in the forest, rather than an open meadow, also helps minimize the impact of your presence since you are less visible.

Hiking the Ice Age Trail across Wisconsin in July included hot and humid days which resulted in heavy dew on some cool mornings. The dew resulted in me having a wet, heavy tent to pack up. When I camped under a tree canopy, much of that dew and condensation was avoided, resulting in faster, easier camp pack-up, and a drier, lighter shelter to carry for many miles through the day.

Tip #28   On cold nights, or nights you expect rain, set the smallest, closed end of your shelter into the prevailing wind direction to reduce air flow through the shelter and stay a bit warmer. Have your shelter's entryway face into the wind for more ventilation and cooling effect on warmer evenings if there is low risk of rain.

Tip #29   If you plan on having a campfire, setting your shelter upwind from the fire will keep you out of the smoke and prevent any rogue spark from melting a hole in your shelter.

Since lightweight synthetic materials melt easily, it does not take much heat to do damage. One of my favorite fleece pull-overs is pock-marked with tiny melt spots from errant campfire sparks. Melted pin pricks in a tent rain cover is even more serious.

Tip #30   When camping at a location that others have previously used, try to reuse the same tent spots that are already worn down. This leaves grasses growing in unused areas to reduce mud creation and minimizes your impact on the site.

Tip #31   When setting up your home for the night in fresh areas, hide your impact as much as possible. Move far enough off trail so others won't see your camp as they walk past. Look for ground cover that is more durable – typically sand, dirt, dead grass, or living grass, in that order.

Many unused areas will have rugged terrain or dense forest, making it difficult to find a suitable camping location. You may need to stop hiking earlier to spend more time locating an adequate spot for the night.

Chapter 5
Nighty Night

If you walk enough days, you'll eventually be so tired you can sleep on a pile of rocks. I think it's better to get a good night's sleep every night by staying comfortable and warm, and minimizing the interruptions to sleep.

Tip #32   Foam ear plugs weigh very little and block out most general camp noise. They may not be enough for the snoring of your tent mate, but an elbow can help with that.

If you use bright colored ear plugs, they can also serve as make-shift fishing bobbers or trail markers. I've also used them as padding to stop clinking of items in my cook kit while I'm hiking.

Tip #33   Make your own pillow for better sleep and a lighter pack. Some people say to use your fleece or down jacket as a pillow, but on cold nights those extra clothes might be needed to stay warm. A bandanna or t-shirt wrapped around a gallon size zip-loc partially filled with air can work fairly well.

I always have my mesh bug suit which I never wear to bed, so I wad it up and wrap it in a bandanna to make a comfortable spot for my head to rest.

Tip #34   A pair of soft, dry socks exclusively for bedtime are a luxury item to consider carrying. They can help keep your quilt or bag clean, warm your feet, and help you sleep. They can also be used in a pinch as mittens, hot pot holders, or for pre-filtering water.

Tip #35   Empty your bladder before bed.

I try to drink my last water of the day no less than 2 hours before hitting the hay. Then, if I use the bathroom just before laying down, I have a better chance of sleeping through the night. Staying warm so your body doesn't shiver also reduces the need to use the toilet during the night.

Tip #36   A sleeping quilt is lighter, smaller, and less expensive than a sleeping bag of equivalent warmth rating. It also allows more freedom to adjust temperature during the night by sticking out a leg or tossing part of it off. The part of a sleeping bag underneath you is compressed and loses much of its insulating benefit. A quilt has no heavy zipper and no extra, compressed insulation so it weighs less and packs smaller for the same amount of effective insulation.

A quilt is a good first "Make Your Own Gear" project to tackle. I've made two synthetic filled quilts, one twice as thick as the other, and I've used them for over ten years now. The last time I used a sleeping bag was on a Kilimanjaro expedition because it was provided by the outfitter, and I didn't have to carry it.

Tip #37   A good sleeping pad is as important as your sleeping bag or quilt for warmth and comfort. There are many pad choices, each with benefits and concerns. Simple closed-cell foam pads are inexpensive, lightweight, and quiet; but they are bulky in your pack and minimally comfortable. Self-inflating pads are more comfortable and a bit warmer, but they are more expensive, heavier, and prone to pinhole leaks. Inflatable pads are lightweight, comfortable, and pack small, but tend to be crinkly, noisy, expensive, and easily punctured.

I've used all kinds of pads and I still switch it up occasionally. Most of the time, I use a cheap, blue foam pad because it's the lightest and most durable. If I'm tight on space or know I'll be camping in less comfortable, rockier spots, I may choose an inflatable pad instead.

Chapter 6
Fear Is Heavy

"Fear Is Heavy" – I've been saying this for over two decades. There are now many variations of the saying that you may have heard.

If I'm afraid of going hungry, I might carry extra food that I don't eat. If I'm afraid of the dark, I might carry extra batteries and a back-up headlamp. If I'm afraid of getting cold, I might carry lots of extra clothes. All this 'extra' weighs me down, slows me down, reduces my fun factor, and is unnecessary.

I say it is unnecessary because of my reasons for bringing it. If I know I eat 1.3 pounds of food each day, I don't really need more than 4 pounds for a 3-day hike. If I put fresh batteries in my headlamp that I've used many times, I know it will last 6 days so I don't need extra batteries. If I research local historic weather and check the forecast, I know what clothes I need. By gathering information and having skills and experience, I eliminate the fear and uncertainty which leads to carrying less unnecessary and redundant equipment.

It is prudent to prepare for the worst and hope for the best, but being realistic about what "the worst" might be is important. Besides reducing your pack weight by leaving out fear-induced redundancy, there are many other ways to lighten up.

Tip #38   Go through every item that you plan to take on a trek. Tell yourself WHY you are taking it. If the reason is "just in case" or "I might need it" then consider leaving it behind. Your first aid kit is one key exception I can think of for this tip.

A corollary to this tip is to ask "What will I do if that reason for taking it does occur and I don't have this item?" If there is a way to improvise a solution with other things in your pack, then consider leaving this item behind.

For example:
- What is the item? A washcloth
- Why take it? So I can wash my body in streams
- What if I don't have it? I can use my bandanna
- Decision? Leave it behind

Tip #39 Hike with a friend. If you are hiking with someone, share as much gear as you can to reduce redundancy and pack weight. You don't both need to carry separate sunscreen, bug spray, stove, water filter, and so on. Many items can be shared, but not your toothbrush or underwear.

Tip #40 Leave your hunting knife, saw, axe, and hatchet at home. These, and all heavy tools, are not needed on hiking adventures.

My hiking knife has a 1.5-inch blade and weighs 1.1oz. I use it to open food packaging, cut string, poke blisters, slice sausage, and other jobs. I can also whittle with it and clean fish. I've never had a need for a big buck knife or heavy multi-tool device. Campfire wood should be small enough to be broken rather than sawed or chopped.

Tip #41   Get a lighter light. A super bright floodlight is not necessary for most hiking trips, and batteries tend to be very heavy items.

My clip-on LED headlamp weighs 0.4oz, including the two tiny, coin batteries that power it for about 20 hours of use. A set of replacement batteries is 0.12oz. That half ounce of weight provides plenty of light for navigating around camp every night for two weeks. In comparison, just one AA battery used in many headlamps weighs about 1 ounce.

Tip #42   Get a light lighter. A BIC lighter is small, but a mini BIC is half the size and still has enough fuel for many weeks of fire starting. Matches are typically not used for lighting cook stoves because they are more difficult to light, weigh more per fire, and get ruined by water.

Tip #43   Repackage consumable materials so only what is needed is taken.

For example, I have a travel size tube of toothpaste I

take on trail. I refill it with the amount of paste I expect to need based on my trek length and leave the big tube at home. You could make dots of toothpaste on plastic wrap and dehydrate it. That falls into the "too much work for little gain" category for me, kind of like cutting off my toothbrush handle, but it might be worth it for you.

Tip #44 Dry your wet gear along the trail during a morning rest break instead of in camp. Your break might take a little longer, but 15 minutes in the sun or wind will reduce the weight quite a bit and make your upcoming night more comfortable and restful.

Wet gear doesn't just come from rain. Moisture constantly leaves your body from breathing and perspiring, and that can condense in your insulating layers. Condensation of the cooler night air can create a fog, shower, or ice storm inside your shelter if conditions are right. So, even after a clear night, your gear may still need airing out.

I try to start hiking as soon as I wake up, while it's still cool. This means I don't hang around for hours in camp waiting for the sun to dry out my gear. Instead, I lay out my shelter, quilt, pad, and anything else that got damp overnight when I take my first long break in the morning's hike. With the sun higher in the sky and air that is warmer, my gear dries faster.

Tip #45   By carrying wet items, such as socks, shelter, or bandanna, in an outer mesh pocket of your backpack, they will dry somewhat while hiking and not get other items wet inside your pack. You could hang wet items off your pack, but I try to never have dangling things since they are easy to lose.

I've found many different items that were dropped along the trail, including: a headlamp, water bottle, hat, camp chair, lone sock, bag of tent stakes, map, and water filter. Their owners did not have a good day.

Tip #46   Leave your wallet at home or hidden in your vehicle and only take your ID, insurance card, one credit card, and 2 $5s, 2 $10s, and 1 $20 on your hike. That cash should be enough for thanking someone for an emergency ride or other predicament you happen to find yourself in.

Tip #47   Leave your heavy key ring in your vehicle and only take your car key on trail. Those keys are just extra weight that is not needed while hiking.

On a 10-day trek across the Philmont Scout Ranch in New Mexico, our route took us through a locked gate. I was trusted to carry the key to that one gate for the entire trek. About 10 minutes of hiking after passing through and re-locking the gate, we took a break and I noticed I no longer had the key.

While the others waited, I hiked back and found the key in the dust by the gate. I had missed when I thought I had dropped it into my pocket. Oops!

Tip #48   Take a month to lose 5 or 10 pounds off YOU before your hike. Nearly all of us can stand to shed that much. Plus, it means your muscles will be in better shape, you'll have more energy, and the hiking will be easier.

My brother gave me just the opposite advice about losing weight. He said that if I gained 30 pounds, then I could just live off the fat for a month and not carry any food. Let me know how that goes for you if you try it.

Tip #49   Get a short haircut before your adventure – it's easier to keep clean and weighs less.

Tip #50   Clip finger and toe nails. OK, it's not much of a weight savings, but carrying a nail clipper is actually more useful than a knife on outings longer than a week. Keeping all your nails clipped helps prevent other problems besides just reducing weight.

I've had the side of a toe rubbed raw before I realized it, and it was caused by a too-long nail on the adjacent toe. I've also had long toe nails wear holes in socks quickly, and long finger nails catch and painfully tear, not to mention the filth that accumulates under them.

Tip #51   Use the toilet in the morning before hiking so you don't carry the extra weight all day. There are fewer bugs and more wildlife out in the early morning, so you might have a chance to comfortably watch animals from your perch and you'll probably have more privacy from other hikers.

Chapter 7
Food Fight

The perfect trail food has high calories, tastes great, weighs little, and is easy to prepare. I continue to try new things as I search for that perfect food.

Food is the second heaviest thing you'll carry on a hike. The only thing worse than carrying too much of it is not carrying enough.

Tip #52   Figure out how much food you'll need for your trek, and carry only that much.

I hate arriving at the end of a trek, or at a resupply town, while I still have a pound or more of food in my pack. It means I just carried that extra weight over dozens of miles for no reason. On the other hand, I was running very low on food with 3 days to the next planned resupply while hiking the Pacific Northwest Trail. I bought $15 worth of candy bars at the Hurricane Ridge visitor center to tide me over to Forks, WA – well, it was actually about $5 worth, but cost a lot more. Running out of food is not fun, and is much worse than having too much.

Most hikers tend to carry more food than they need. A typical adult burns around 60 calories per hour just sitting around. It takes about 70 calories to move 100 pounds 1 mile along a trail. If you and your pack weigh a total of 200 pounds, that's 140 calories per mile. If you plan to go on a 20-day hike, covering 300 miles, you'll need about 140*300=42,000 calories for the hiking effort to cover that distance.

If you hike about 15 miles per day at about 2 miles per hour, you'll hike 8 hours and rest 16 hours each day. That's another 16 hours * 60 cal/hour * 20 days =

19,200 calories for a total calorie need of 61,200 for the entire trek. That is a bit over 3,000 calories per day. I bet that is less than you expected you would need to hike 15 miles a day.

Tip #53   Choose calorie-dense food. The more calorie dense food you eat, the less food weight you need to carry. One ounce of vegetable oil has around 240 calories while one ounce of broccoli has   10 calories. I could carry 10 ounces of oil or 15 pounds of broccoli for one day of hiking. In reality, you can't live off just oil so a mix of food is needed. You also can't live off just broccoli.

When you combine all the carbohydrates, proteins, and fats that you plan to eat, a common goal is to average around 125 calories per ounce. Anything over that is bonus fuel for free! If we had 125cal/oz food in our 61,200 calorie example earlier, that would be about 30 pounds of food to hike 300 miles over 20 days – or 1.5 pounds per day.

Tip #54   Repackage food to reduce trash and weight. If the food is already in a lightweight bag, like bagels or tortillas, then repackaging doesn't make sense, but the cardboard boxes around pop-tarts, crackers, and the like, are just extra weight to be recycled at home. Taking a box of 12 granola bars just because they're packed that way when you only need 4 is extra weight that you'll carry the entire distance.

As an experiment when preparing for a week-long trek with a group of 10 people, I weighed all the packaging we left at home to see if it really mattered. It wound up being a little more than 10% of the total weight, and that seems significant to me.

Tip #55   Cook outside your shelter – even if it's cold, or rainy, or windy, or late, or early. Don't use those excuses to cook inside your tent because spilling food makes a mess and attracts animals, hot metal easily melts shelter and clothing fabric, and noxious fumes could build up and become dangerous.

Tip #56   Graze all day – eat small amounts throughout the day rather than a few big meals. This keeps a steady fuel supply to your engine which helps you maintain a nice hiking pace all day.

I try to eat something every hour or so to keep my energy level up. When my little bag of snacks is empty, it's time to stop and get more snacks from my pack.

Tip #57   Shop around for your food. There are significant price differences for identical foods between stores. It pays to shop around before buying a few weeks' or months' worth of food items.

I've found that Aldi or Walmart are wonderful for high-calorie, inexpensive food for long hikes.

Tip #58   Zip-loc bags work well for repackaging. They are sturdy, lightweight, and inexpensive. They can also be washed and reused many times instead of thrown out after a single use.

I use sandwich size bags for loose food, such as candies, nuts, powders, and dried fruit. Quart size bags are good for dehydrated meals. Gallon or 2.5 gallon sizes work great for holding the all smaller food bags inside my backpack.

Tip #59   Dehydrate your own food instead of buying it. By investing in an inexpensive home dehydrator, you can dry everything from apricots to zucchini, saving weight and space.

I've dried jerky, fruit leather, spaghetti sauce, and my favorite – cantaloupe.

Tip #60   Eat food that requires no cooking. Packing pouches of chicken or tuna, crackers, bars, sausage, and the like means you don't need to carry a stove, fuel, and cooking gear. It also saves a lot of time that is not spent cooking and cleaning, and you can stop for a food break whenever and wherever you want.

If you just can't live without your mocha coffee caffeine fix, consider trying chocolate-covered coffee beans instead of carrying all the gear needed to brew a cup.

Tip #61   Another option to cooking is "cold soaking". Put your dried food in a sealed container with water and let it sit there in your pack for hours while you hike. Eventually, it is re-hydrated and edible, just not hot.

This has worked best for me on solo hikes but not with groups because some people don't like the idea of eating cold food that is supposed to be hot. Before deciding to do this on a long hike, I recommend you try it a few times at home to ensure the meals taste good to you.

Tip #62   If you do cook, or cold soak, consider purchasing large containers of freeze-dried meats and vegetables, store-bought instant potatoes and noodles, and spices to make your own meals. Buying all the bulk dried ingredients and making your own meals cuts the price almost in half and allows for custom combinations of flavors.

Now that my wife has been joining me on hikes for the past few years, we have been assembling our own dried meals. By re-hydrating the meals in reusable bags, our pot is only used to heat water. Having hot food is great, having no clean up is wonderful, and saving money is terrific.

Tip #63   A can of Pringles potato chips might be the best food item ever. The chips are tasty, lightweight, and calorie dense. Share them with hikers you meet to guarantee instant friendships. They make great fire-starting tinder since they have so much oil in them. Plus, the cardboard tube makes a great trash can.

After eating all the chips, I like to see how many days' worth of trash I can compress into the can – I've gotten 6 days of garbage into 1 can. I rarely go on a multi-day hike without a can in my pack.

Tip #64   Protein powder is a fast, easy, and lightweight way to get protein calories. Protein rich foods tend to be less calorie dense, but are needed to ensure that you are consuming protein to repair muscles when hiking.

At the end of a day's hike while I'm preparing dinner, I often enjoy a half liter water bottle with chocolate protein powder mixed in. Nuts and seeds, jerky, cheese, and beans are other protein foods that I enjoy on trail.

Tip #65   Since drinking vegetable oil straight out of the bottle is not a viable solution for ingesting calories, high-fat spreads such as Nutella, peanut butter, and almond butter are good alternatives. They are easy, tasty, and packed with fat calories.

Nut spreads allow your body to digest the calories in the nuts more efficiently than eating whole nuts. The same calories of peanut butter weighs about the same as whole, shelled peanuts, but takes up less space and more of the calories get used by your body.

A small jar of nut spread feels very heavy because it is so dense, but it is very calorie-efficient weight.

Tip #66 Eat a substantial meal after a day of hiking so your body can process the calories through the night and work on your muscles.

I often follow dinner with a handful of sunflower seeds and a candy bar just before brushing my teeth as the last thing in the evening. This gives my body some calories to burn through the night.

Tip #67 A daily multi-vitamin helps ensure your body is receiving nutrients which may be lacking in all those high calorie foods you're eating.

Tip #68 Eat what you like. It makes no sense to pack anything that you won't enjoy eating, so choose food that sounds good.

Here's a starter list of food to consider:
- kale, asparagus, cauliflower – Just Kidding!
- Peanut M&Ms, Snickers
- Sunflower kernels, almonds, macadamia nuts, pecans, pumpkin seeds, peanut butter, hazelnut spread
- Summer sausage, salami, jerky, spam, tuna or salmon or chicken pouches
- Hard cheese, dried fruit, pop-tarts, dark chocolate, shredded coconut
- Ritz crackers, Austin crackers, Pringles, Fritos

- Gummy worms, Sour Patch Kids, Little Debbie desserts, Oreos
- If you're going to cold soak or cook: oatmeal, ramen, instant potatoes, Knorr noodles or rice, couscous
- Tuna packs come in tons of flavors – chipotle, teriyaki, chili, ... & others

Tip #69   Minimize cost per calorie: If you don't care how much your long hike will cost, just skip this one. There are expensive calories and cheap calories. For example, almonds have about 170 calories per ounce and cost $10/lb while peanuts have about 165 calories per ounce but cost $3/lb. That's a 3x price difference for similar calories and weight cost. I'd go with peanuts because I consider both weight per calorie and cost per calorie.

Tip #70   If you're sure you will eat a lot of a particular food item, such as jerky or chocolate, buy it in bulk to save money, and check online stores for more savings.

Plan ahead and buy food during sales. The challenge then is to not dip into your hiking stash of tasty food before your big hike.

For example, I know I will be buying a couple

pounds of peanut M&Ms for a hike and they have a very long shelf life. So, a few months before my hike, I start checking sales and make the purchase when I find a significant savings.

Tip #71   Eat on the trail. There's no rule that says you must eat your dinner at your campsite.

If I plan to hike until sunset before stopping for the day, which I often do on summer days with long sunlight hours, I will eat my dinner along the trail. This lets me take a stop at a scenic spot, get another rest break, and reduce food smells at my camping location.

When I'm eating a non-cook breakfast, such as granola bars or pop-tarts, I put it in my right pants pocket, pack up all my gear and I'm on the trail in about 15 minutes. When I get hungry, whether that's 5 minutes or 50 minutes later, I just eat on the trail. This saves a lot of time, gets more cool morning miles in, and gets me moving sooner rather than sitting around camp being chilly while eating. As a bonus, it helps keep campsites clear of food micro-trash.

Tip #72   Share your trail snacks with a hiking partner. The sooner your food is eaten, the less your pack weighs and your partner winds up carrying their heavy food longer. Your plan is that they will share with you later. Just hope they don't figure it out too soon, or you might be hungry at the end.

When my wife and I hike, we usually eat all her snacks first. This makes her pack lighter quickly so we can travel more efficiently as a team.

Chapter 8
H2O

"No spit, no sweat, no need to go? Fix it all with H2O!" I came up with that saying for a contest a few years ago and won a water bottle for my efforts. Whoop!

Staying hydrated in the wild is a critical skill. In general, we should all drink more water than we do every day, but on trail getting a drink of water takes much more effort than just turning a faucet and waiting for the water to get cold.

Tip #73   Treat all drinking water that does not come right out of a reliable potable source, such as a faucet. Crystal clear water can still be contaminated. Always, always, ALWAYS treat water before drinking it! It is a simple, easy process that takes very little time, and the potential problems from drinking non-treated water far outweigh the small effort to treat it before drinking.

Water can be manually filtered, treated with chemicals, boiled, or zapped with UV light to make it safe to ingest. I have used a Sawyer Squeeze manual filter for the past 12 years because it is lightweight, easy, effective, and inexpensive. Water that has been manually filtered has the dangerous bacteria removed while the other three methods just kill it, but it remains in the water so you still ingest it. Whatever you do, treat your water! I always do, and I've never gotten sick from bad water.

Tip #74   Camel Up – drink your fill of treated water at the source and then only carry enough with you to the next known source, or as far as you want to hike until stopping for water. It's less effort to carry water in your body than in a bottle.

If I drink about 1 liter of water right after treating it from the source, I can typically hike for about 5 or 6 miles, or 2 hours, before needing another drink. On trails with many water sources, carrying ½ liter of water is all that is necessary.

Tip #75   Be familiar with the trail ahead of you so you know how far the next water source is. This means you should carry, and be able to read, a topographic map, or have hiked the trail before. Knowing how much water you typically need to consume in order to cover a distance, and knowing the distance to the next water, tells you how much water you need to carry.

North of Flagstaff, the Arizona Trail has a section of almost 60 miles with no reliable water sources. I would need to carry around 20 pounds of water to cover that distance safely. Fortunately, a friend in Flagstaff cached a gallon jug of water for me under a bush halfway along the section so I only carried 8 pounds of water at the most.

Tip #76   Worse than carrying too much food is carrying too much water. Water is the heaviest item you will carry, but also the most important, so carry enough, but not much more than you will need until your next water source.

For example, the trail may cross a stream every 1 or 2 miles, but I know I can hike 10 miles with 1 liter of water after drinking up. I would rather carry 2 pounds of water for 10 miles than stop 3 or 4 times along that distance to get more water. Conversely, I don't want to load up with 12 pounds of water just so I can hike a 30-mile day without stopping to collect more.

Tip #77   A comfortable, consistent pace helps hikers consume less water and calories. Pounding your way up and down hills, huffing and puffing and sweating, might gain you a few extra miles in a day but you'll probably need to stop more often for water and you may need to carry more food. These extra stops and extra carried weight will offset the gains you might get from hiking harder. Only you can decide how fast "comfortable" is for you, but in general you should be able to have a conversation while hiking, and not have sweat beading on your face.

Tip #78   Disposable plastic water bottles are good containers for carrying water. They are easy to replace and can be used multiple times. They are light, durable, and inexpensive compared to other bottles, bags, and containers hikers use to hold water.

I use two 600ml disposables to carry only water. I typically use them for a few months, and I've not had one break yet.

If needed, I can also carry another 2 liters of water in the dirty water bag that is used with my Sawyer Squeeze water filter. I'm carrying the bag anyway, so it's no extra weight.

Tip #79   Tannins in water give it a brownish color, and an earthy odor and taste, but it is safe. Most portable water treatment methods will not remove tannins, so your filtered water still looks like tea. This is a common concern of new hikers, but tannins are not a health concern. Just drink the water.

Sediment in water makes it murky which is different than tannins. A glass of tannin water is clear but off color, like a weak tea. Some of our rivers with rapids in northern Minnesota look like rivers of root beer with foam on top in the eddies.

Tip #80   A pinch of electrolyte powder or drop of concentrated flavor liquid is a great way to help you drink more water on hikes, especially if the treated water doesn't look, smell, or taste like what you're used to at home.

Whenever I lead a group on a trek, I always bring some Gatorade powder just in case someone dislikes the water taste. If it's just me, I don't bring it because I'll drink pretty much any filtered water since I trust my filter to do its job.

Tip #81   Gather water in the evening, but drink it in the morning. If you have time, fill your water containers at the end of the day at camp before it gets too dark and they will be chilly cold by morning.

When I start hiking for the day, I drink as much as I can before leaving camp, and top off my water bottles. This way, I start well hydrated. Drinking a lot before bed may mean a poor night's sleep interrupted by a few toilet visits. Taking a few breaks along the trail in the morning after drinking a lot is no big deal.

Tip #82   Carry about a half liter of water in an uncontaminated container, such as an extra bottle, flask, or bag, in case it is needed for something other than your personal consumption.

If I'm hiking with others, I never drink from one of my two water bottles that only holds clean water. If my drinking bottle becomes empty, I pour water from the safe one into the one I drink from. This allows me to share the water in the non-drink bottle, or use it for first aid, or any other reason that needs clean water. I mark the bottle lid with an X so I know which one to use and which one to keep clean.

SHT4U2NO

Chapter 9
Toiletiquette

Proper pooping is of paramount importance. Natural bodily functions continue to happen when out in nature. Without the easy privacy and hygiene we're used to in civilization, some new skills and practices make using the 'toilet' easier and more efficient.

Tip #83   Plan your poop so you have time to do a good job. Waiting until it's inevitable will mean having a more frantic and less enjoyable experience, so start planning your poop as soon as you start feeling a need.

Tip #84   Use established toilets whenever possible. On many maintained trails, public shelters or campsites with toilets are also maintained. Even if you don't plan on camping there, using the toilet as you pass by makes life much easier.

When a long trail passes through a park, campground, or town, I am sure to make use of a public bathroom. After improvising toilets for a week, it's a luxury to enjoy a flushing toilet and a sink with running water.

Tip #85   Dig a cat hole and bury your poop if there are no toilets around.

These are general guidelines specifically for cat holes:
- At least 70 full steps away from any water source, trail, or campsite
- Between 6 and 9 inches deep
- Large enough to hold all of the waste

- Bury used toilet paper
- Cover the used hole with the removed dirt to restore the area
- Know the local regulations which may override these guidelines

Tip #86   You don't need to aim and hit the hole, that's too difficult. Just do your business and then push it into the hole with a stick.

Tip #87   Guys, pee before you squat to poop to keep your pants dry and splash free.

Tip #88   Save toilet paper by collecting some big, soft leaves to use for the main wiping and just use toilet paper for finishing. Knowing what kinds of plants are in the area is helpful.

Tip #89   Try to get as comfortable as possible. Squatting works anywhere, but can tire out your legs.

I prefer to sit on a log with my rear hanging over the back side. You can also hold onto a tree, lean against a large rock, or even use your hiking poles for support.

Tip #90   Poop in the morning so you don't carry the extra weight hiking all day. There are fewer active insects to bother you in the cool morning, too. You might even get to see some wildlife while quietly taking care of business out in the woods all alone.

I've had deer, turkeys, and squirrels walk past me in the early morning as I sat quietly on a log.

Tip #91   Poop in the woods. The ground in a forest tends to be better digging than above timberline or open areas which are rockier and offer less privacy.

Tip #92   Plan to hike a few minutes away from camp to poop, not just behind the nearest bush. It's a good idea to take a friend or at least let others know you're heading out.

I once had someone in our group turn the wrong way when they got back to the trail after using a permanent outdoor toilet and was lost for almost an hour before getting back to camp. Another time, someone went into a small clump of trees and then walked out the other side of it when finished. They were disoriented for a few minutes before figuring out the direction back to camp.

Tip #93   Keep all your toilet items in a small waterproof kit that's easy to get to in your backpack.

Mine is a 1-gallon zip-loc bag that contains toilet paper in a smaller zip-loc, a digging trowel, and a tiny bottle of alcohol-based hand sanitizer in a zip-loc. I estimate 12 squares of TP per day when resupplying my kit.

Tip #94   Follow the toilet rules. As more areas receive more human traffic, regulations are being put in place to combat the human waste problem. Know the regulations where you're going, which may include packing out toilet paper and even your poop.

Personally, I avoid visiting any areas with these strict regulations because they already have too many people impacting the area.

SHT4U2NO

Chapter 10
Crushing It

Backpacking campers tend to carry their gear to a destination and then camp there for a few days, doing other activities such as fishing, climbing, or day hikes. Long distance hikers have hiking as their main activity every day of their trek. In order to complete a long trail, significant miles need to be covered every day.

Tip #95   Start your day of hiking early. Every hour of daylight that passes while you sip coffee, lounge around, break camp, or wait for your tent to dry is a couple miles you won't hike this day. By waking up with the sun, you have more hours of hiking each day.

It's light enough to see just fine a half hour before sunrise for an even earlier start. A sunrise is often more beautiful than a sunset because the weather is calmer and more clear in the early morning. There are typically fewer insects and people awake, but more animals sharing all the spectacular views with you. For a bonus, early morning hours tend to be cooler which tends to be nicer for hiking.

Tip #96   Hike longer, not faster. Everyone has their own comfortable pace that most effortlessly covers distance.

If I have to hike too slowly in a group, I get worn out from the monotony, trudging along at a snail's pace. If I have to push myself to keep up with someone, that tires me out also. An awkward pace also increases the probability of blisters, joint injuries, and muscle strains.

Rather than pushing myself to hike 4mph for 6 hours and being wiped out with sore legs the next day, I can cover the same distance travelling 3mph for 8 hours and remain able to do those 24 miles day after day.

One resupply spot on the Arizona Trail is a marina on Lake Roosevelt, and they are only open from 8am to 4pm. I was still about 15 miles away at noon, so I sped ahead of my hiking partner and reached the marina with about 15 minutes to spare. Sometimes, you DO just need to hike faster.

Tip #97 Keep moving. When you're not moving, you're not covering miles. Rather than stopping for a leisurely 10 minute snack break, you could eat your snack while just sauntering along at only a half mile an hour and still travel some distance for those 10 minutes.

On steeper uphills, my pace might slow way down but I do my best to continue moving. I've found that stopping on an uphill is very demoralizing for me, and more difficult to start up again. I do my best to not stop until I get to the top of any ascent, or at least to a false summit with a flat section of trail.

Tip #98   Shorten breaks. It's easy to sit and enjoy a great view for a half hour, but the view has been seen and a few photos taken in the first five minutes. The other 20+ minutes was another mile that could have been hiked.

Walking along at a casual pace can be as much of a rest as sitting, and the view gradually changes from each vantage point. Keeping breaks short also helps prevent leg muscles from cooling down and getting tight.

Tip #99   Improve efficiency. Prioritizing all the tasks you need to take care of at each hiking break makes your breaks more efficient, resulting in more hiking time.

My tasks, in this order, tend to be: use toilet, get water, rest legs, check location on map. After using the toilet, if I need to, I sit and filter my water while resting my legs and checking the map. A stop rarely needs to take more than 15 minutes every couple hours, but it certainly can if you just want to relax awhile.

The same ordering of tasks for efficiency is true for morning and evening routines. Consistency and efficiency work together to minimize wasted time.

Every morning, packing up camp in the same way with every item getting packed in the same spot in your backpack makes setting up camp at night faster. Organizing your gear at camp the same way every night makes breaking camp easier the next morning.

I'm often looking for more efficient ways to pack and ways to make the camp set up and break down process smoother, but after a week on trail you'll probably have it pretty well dialed in.

By keeping common items in consistent locations, it takes less time and effort to use them. My water bottle is always on my front pack strap, phone is in my right hip pocket, filter in left pack pocket, ... I don't have to expend mental effort remembering where an item is, nor worry if it's been misplaced. When I need something, I can quickly get it and use it.

Tip #100   Leave Your Pack On. When taking a short rest break, find a rock or log to sit on that will take the weight of your pack off your body. This lets you get a quick rest without the time and effort of dropping your pack all the way to the ground and lifting it back up. It also helps keep the break short and makes starting up again easier.

Tip #101   Keep fueling the motor. A big breakfast and dinner is fine for home life, but a steady flow of incoming energy works better when you are exercising your muscles from sun-up to sun-down. A pouch or pocket full of snacks that can be easily eaten throughout the day provides the required calories.

One of my biggest ongoing shortcomings as a hiker is my failure to eat enough during the day. I enjoy the hiking so much that I forget to eat, or fail to take the time to eat. So, I use the right leg pocket of my pants to hold bars and bags of snacks. I use the left pocket as a trash bag. I try to make sure I eat something often.

Tip #102   Care for your legs. Whenever there's a hiking break for more than 15 minutes, take some time to rest with your legs elevated – on a log, rock, or your pack. Stretch your leg muscles at breaks and in camp immediately at the end of the day's hike to help prevent stiffness and soreness.

Chapter 11
Thrifty, Not Cheap

Most people see hiking as a very inexpensive activity. After all, you're just walking. That's true – walking is practically free – but multi-day hiking treks can actually be more expensive than normal life if you aren't careful. Money spent on equipment, food, transportation to the trail, and town stops all adds up.

By now, you've probably figured out that I'm cheap – just ask my wife. Actually, part of the adventure of long-distance hiking for me is to do it as inexpensively as possible and still enjoy myself.

If you have money to burn and don't care about reducing the cost of your long hike, skip ahead now. Otherwise, these few tips can help save you significant money over the span of a long hike.

Tip #103   Buy food at low-cost grocery stores before your hike. I've found that both Walmart and Aldi win with high-calorie, low-cost food that is perfect for long hikes. You probably have similar stores near you.

Hiking the Florida Trail, I discovered that Publix is pretty much the most common grocery store around in Florida so I knew I could get a good selection of items there.   There may be an inexpensive regional store chain where you're planning to hike that would be a good bet.

Tip #104   Planning where to purchase your food in trail towns before you get there can save money. If a town that is 6 days down the trail has a big grocery store and the town 5 days away only has a small convenience store, I might start hiking with an extra day of food. I'd carry more weight but get a better selection of food at lower prices. Or, I might decide to buy only a few items at the convenience store just to get me to the next town. That would mean an extra stop, but it could be worth it.

Passing through the Big Cypress Reservation on the Florida Trail, I figured I needed two more days of food to reach the next town. The only place I could find with any groceries was a gas station. It was probably the most expensive resupply I ever had because I didn't plan well enough.

Tip #105   MYOG! – if you Make Your Own Gear, you can save lots of money and have keen knowledge of your gear before hitting the trail. Some items, such as hiking shoes, don't make much sense to make yourself, but things like quilts, clothes, lightweight packs, and some utensils are expensive to buy and not very hard to make.

I have two quilts and two packs that I made and use all the time. I also have a ton of MacGyvered items that I've created from old things that I've repurposed. Some examples: my food cozy made from an old sleeping pad, mosquito mittens from an old tent screen, sun gloves from old liner socks, and a filter attachment from two bottle lids.

Tip #106   Buying used or off-brand items can be a big money saver. Personally, I wouldn't buy someone's used toothbrush, underwear, socks, or shoes, but a pack, stove, or down jacket that hasn't been used much could be a good deal. Maybe someone bought it for their thru-hike attempt but stopped after a week and now it is no longer needed. Or, someone is upgrading to the latest version and their old item is still completely usable.

There are many online used gear groups, local second-hand stores, college outdoor programs, and rental shops that cycle out old equipment.

My son is an expert at this. He put together a complete mountaineering outfit almost entirely from used gear he found online.

Tip #107   Hike more miles in fewer days. Every day of hiking costs more money. By hiking more miles each day, you are on trail fewer days and that costs less. All the tips in the "Crushing It" section address ways to do this.

Tip #108   Carefully manage the Love/Hate relationship with trail towns. Every long trail passes through or near towns. They are wonderful for resupplying food, taking a day off trail, and getting rested and rejuvenated. They are also a money pit that can easily double the cost of any trek.

After completing our Border Route Trail thru-hike, my wife and I decided to spend the night in Grand Marais, MN rather than drive home the same day we got off trail. The hotel, meals, and evening out cost more than our 10 days of hiking, but it was a great way to celebrate our success.

Remember to be conscious of your expenses in town and consider the following specific tips about typical splurges.

Tip #109   Skip alcohol, or at least minimize it. Purchasing alcohol from a store rather than a bar or restaurant is much cheaper and more convenient. If you do buy alcohol to take on the trail, choose plastic bottles instead of glass since they weigh less and won't break in your pack.

I don't carry alcohol on the trail, but many hikers

do. I consider having a beer in a trail town a great reward for the days of exertion to get there.

Tip #110   Limit restaurant meals. Buy food at grocery stores for most of your in-town meals. It saves all the expense of paying others to cook and clean for you. This is especially useful if you are a small group of hikers. Ingredients for a dozen big sandwiches are much cheaper than purchasing 12 pre-made ones.

Tip #111   Eat your fruits and veggies. While you're in town, eat all the heavy, healthy, fresh food that you wouldn't carry on trail because it is not very calorie dense.

Tip #112   AYCE is a hiker's best town friend. All You Can Eat meals, whether Chinese, pizza, or a buffet, are a perfect way to pack thousands of calories into your starving body.

I sat in a Chinese AYCE for three hours one afternoon in a trail town on the Ice Age Trail, taking my time eating everything until I couldn't stuff in another egg roll. I sure didn't hike very far out of town that night, but was very well energized for the next long day.

Tip #113   Camp instead of staying in a hotel. Some towns have campgrounds or parks where you can stay, especially if you've contacted the city before arriving. You might also get lucky and meet a local resident willing to take you in for a night.

On the Ice Age Trail, I stopped at the one bar in a small town for dinner and asked about a place to camp. The bartender called the mayor and got permission for me to lay out my sleeping bag in the amphitheater in the local park.

Also on the Ice Age Trail, I met a woman on the street in a tiny Wisconsin town and she invited me to spend the night with her family. This has actually happened at least once on every long hike I've done. These home stays often include a dinner, breakfast, and shower, saving even more money. They are sweet surprises of Trail Magic, but hikers should not expect them to happen.

Tip #114   Do NEROs rather than ZEROs. A Zero day is a day spent hiking zero miles of the trail. It's a day usually spent in a trail town washing clothes, buying food, and visiting AYCEs. It also often means a hotel stay, hopefully with a hot shower, comfortable bed, and good WiFi.

Many hikers will hike a long day and arrive in town in the evening, get a hotel room for the night, stay there a second night after doing all their in-town chores, and then hike out the next morning. That's two nights lodging expense for just one day of rest.

Another option is to plan your day's hike to end a couple miles from the edge of town and camp there. Then, start early in the morning, do a short hike into town, get your place to stay, and do all your chores. Enjoy the evening, sleep well, and enjoy as much of the next day in town that you want. Hike out of town later in the day to reach the next close camping spot. By doing this, you have two very short hiking days (called NEROs because they are Nearly Zeros) with almost two days of rest for the cost of only one night in town.

Chapter 12
Bite, Scratch, & Itch

Living out in nature for an extended time means you will meet many of the animals, insects, and plants that live there. It's a treat to encounter some of these, but others tend to just be nuisances. Expecting them, and planning your protection, is key to a positive hike.

Spray or lotion can temporarily repel insects, but

you will sweat off the chemicals soon enough and probably wind up getting some of it in your eyes, eating some of it, rolling in it in your sleeping bag, and contaminating water sources whenever you wash. For those reasons, I prefer other ways to avoid the little critters.

Spiders are the bane of hiking in forests. Meeting a tall hiker coming toward me on the trail is always a reason for celebration because I know that for the next couple hours I will have web-free hiking. Those spiders can spin new webs faster than I can hike, so it's only a matter of time before the silky tendrils are back across the trail. The only thing worse than a face full of spider web is a face full of spider! Fortunately, these spiders that spin face-high webs are not dangerously venomous so they are mostly just a nuisance.

Tip #115   If you aren't in a hurry or don't need to cover many miles, wait for some other hiker to leave your camping area first. Let them clear the webs. Following a tall hiker is even better.

Both the Appalachian Trail and Ice Age Trail are tied for 'Webbiest' trail in my opinion. Being 6' 1", even following other hikers often doesn't help since most are shorter than me.

Tip #116   A mesh bug net hat makes a great web catcher. They are intended to protect from mosquitoes and other flying insect bites, but I will wear one even if there are no mosquitoes out if the spider webs are thick.

Tip #117   Waving a hiking pole or stick a few feet out in front of your face will catch most of the spider webs before your face reaches them.

I've done this plenty of times but it's a bit of extra work. It is fun to hold the pole up in the sun after awhile to see all the streamers hanging off it.

Tip #118   Keeping zippers closed on your shelter at all times is a great way to keep your portable home bug-free, snake-free, and rodent-free.

Ticks are disgusting tiny arachnids, especially when they are bloated with blood. Their bite doesn't hurt, but they are more dangerous than spiders due to the diseases they may carry. Do some research to know if you are hiking in tick territory or not.

Tip #119   Treating clothing with permethrin prevents almost all tick bites, as long as you wear the clothes.

I treat all my hiking clothes except underwear at the start of hiking season. I also treat my backpack and shelter.

Tip #120   Since ticks take awhile to bite in and start feeding, checking your entire body for ticks every morning and evening should keep you safe and healthy. It sure doesn't hurt to check at other times such as using the toilet or swimming.

Tip #121   Removing embedded ticks should be done with a tweezers, or check out a Tick Key product – no squeezing, just a simple lifting of the tick.

Mosquitoes are the worst. I can avoid ticks and spiders, but mosquitoes can be an incessant nuisance, and nearly impossible to escape.

Tip #122   Ending your day of hiking before sunset may be all that is required to avoid the mosquito problem.

On the Florida Trail, there were absolutely no mosquitoes during the day. As soon as the sun reached the horizon they swarmed mercilessly for about 90 minutes, and then disappeared again. Setting up my shelter and resting inside at that time solved the problem nicely.

Tip #123   If you're going to bed early, then you might as well start hiking early. If you are on the move by sunrise, mosquitoes tend to be much less of a bother, but then there are still those early morning spider webs.

Tip #124   When mosquitoes are out during the day, the best way to stay sane is to keep moving. They tend to swarm around more when you stop for a rest break, making you an easier target.

I've had many days when I could hear and see the swarm of mosquitoes following in my wake. I often wonder how far a mosquito will follow potential prey before giving up. The best answer I could figure out from research is about a quarter mile, but usually much less. And, they can fly at about 1.5 mph so a brisk hiking pace keeps you just out of their reach.

Tip #125   Taking breaks in open, sunny areas is best. The air tends to be a bit drier and there's a better chance of a breeze that will make the mosquitoes work harder to attack.

Tip #126   There are really two solutions to all these insect problems. The first is to just hike in the winter. When it's cold enough, you won't be bothered at all by the hordes of pests.

In Minnesota, I look forward to the first real frost in the fall because insect activity drops dramatically after that happens.

Tip #127   The other solution, which I use, is to keep a physical barrier between you and the insects. I have a mesh bug jacket with hood, mesh pants, and mesh mittens (that I made myself). The entire setup weighs about 7 ounces. Fortunately, no one really cares what your outfit looks like on trail since function is much more important than fashion.

One comment I hear more than any other (by far) from people I meet on my hikes is about my bug suit. The comment is nearly always the same - "Wow! What cool pants!" or "Hey, now that's smart!"

Tip #128   Mesh bug suits do a great job of keeping mosquitoes and ticks at bay, but they also:

- Protect legs from scratchy, prickly, itchy plants
- Protect face from spider webs
- Protect from biting flies that ignore bug spray
- Go on and off as needed, no reapplying every few hours
- Leave no chemicals on your skin
- Weigh about 7 ounces
- Make a great pillow when wrapped inside a bandanna

Depending on where you hike, plants can be as serious a nuisance as insects. On the Arizona Trail, every plant scratched, cut, or poked me. There were no soft, gentle plants. Luckily, none of them were poisonous so infection from the cuts getting dirty was the biggest real concern.

Tip #129   The best protection from sharp plants is cloth. Long pants and long-sleeved shirts do the job just fine with the trade-off of a hotter hike.

Hiking across Costa Rica, there was a type of long grass with barbed tips that could easily draw blood as I walked past. I wore long pants the entire time and could feel the grass snag at the cloth often. Better the pants than my legs.

Tip #130   Wash your clothes as soon as possible after a hike. Most trails across the country have many opportunities for encountering poison ivy and other troublesome plants. Long pants help protect your legs from rubbing against poisonous plants, but the oils stay on the pants and will eventually get to your skin unless they are washed away.

Tip #131   Stay on established trails. Vigilance and recognizing these plants so you can avoid them is best. Most popular trails will have a tread wide enough that you won't rub against them if you stay on the trail. Leaving the trail to camp, use the toilet, or get water, requires a close eye to pick a safe route.

Chapter 13
They Went That-a-way

Hiking is a simple sport, but knowing where you are and ensuring you are walking the correct direction can be challenging. With evolving technology, navigation gets easier every year, yet every year hikers continue to get lost out in the wild. Navigation skills are important whether you're using the latest phone app or going old school with a paper map and compass. If your batteries die or your map falls out of your pack somewhere far behind you on the trail, knowing a few ways to estimate direction can be very valuable.

Tip #132 Know Your Blazes. A blaze is a marker showing where the trail goes. They are typically about the size of a dollar bill painted on trees, but you can still see antique blazes chopped into trees with an ax on some remote trails. They also may be painted on bedrock, light posts, guardrails, the back of a stop sign, or any convenient spot along the trail.

There is no international (or national) standard for blazes, so know the blazes for the trail you're hiking. On the Superior Hiking Trail, a blue blaze marks the main trail and a white blaze indicates a spur trail. On the Appalachian Trail, a white blaze marks the main trail and a blue blaze is a spur trail. Ice Age Trail blazes are yellow. Florida Trail blazes are orange. Pacific Northwest Trail blazes are invisible – really, I saw only a handful along the entire trail but it's gradually getting better marked. Across the desert on the Arizona Trail, blazes were on composite posts planted in the barren ground. In Europe, long trails use red and white blazes.

I stood in front of one tree on the Florida Trail that had blue, orange, yellow, and white blazes painted on it – how confusing! It just happened to be an intersection of four separate trails in the area.

Tip #133   Learn to speak Topo – that's the language of a "topographic" map with lines, colors, numbers, and symbols showing important navigation information. Most people now use electronic devices for navigation, but understanding topographic representations is still important on both digital and physical navigation devices – that would be both phones and paper maps.

Tip #134   Contour lines show changes in elevation on topographic maps. If these lines are close together, it means a steep area; far apart means relatively flat. This helps plan the difficulty and time required for upcoming trail sections.

A destination on the map may look to be a short, straight path from your current location, but a longer path around a steep mountain or deep canyon may actually be much safer, easier, and faster than a straight shot.

Tip #135   Know your map's scale. 1 inch might represent 1 mile or 10 miles. It might not look far to the next campsite, but may take forever to reach it.

There are many ways to use nature to help with navigation. I may not look at my map or phone app for half a day as long as I'm confident that I'm on trail. Some of the ways to read nature are simple and fast, but they are for general direction, not precise bearings such as a compass provides.

These nature navigation tips are for the northern hemisphere. There are different constellations in the southern hemisphere, and the sun and moon are generally in the north when hiking 'down under'. If you are in the southern hemisphere, just switch 'north' and 'south' wherever they appear in the next few tips.

Tip #136   A general feeling for sun location is important. If I'm hiking northbound, then I should see my shadow ahead of me and the sun's heat should generally be on my back. If I notice the sun is in my eyes, I should stop and check my map. The same is true with shadows of trees around me – the shadows should be pointing the same general direction I'm hiking. If my trail is westward, then the sun is behind me in the morning and ahead of me in the afternoon, but it is generally always over my left shoulder which is to the south.

The same general rule is true for the moon whether it's up during the night or day. It will be generally to the south since it travels roughly the same path as the sun.

Tip #137   Viewing constellations of stars is an entertaining way to end a day of hiking. Being able to find the north star from both the Big Dipper and Cassiopeia allows you to know your general direction for night hiking. If nothing else, you can mark North in the dirt at your campsite to help ensure you start out in the correct direction in the morning. It's not uncommon for tired hikers to accidentally set out the wrong direction in the early morning, racking up miles going back down the trail they just hiked in on.

Tip #138   The horn tips of a partial moon point south.

Looking at the moon, draw an imaginary line from the highest horn down to the lower horn. Continue to follow that line down, down, down to the horizon and that is roughly south. It still works when the moon is greater than half-full, as long as you can see where the upper and lower points are on the moon.

Tip #139   If you have an hour to spare, the movement of the sun's shadow can point the way east and west.

Find a flat area of dirt or sand that has no shadows on it from trees or bushes. Smooth the area a bit and stand a 2 foot long stick up in the center of it. Mark the exact end of the stick's shadow with a small pebble. 15 or 20 minutes later, mark the new end of the shadow. Repeat this a third time. This line of pebbles runs east-west with the first pebble being west and the last being east.

Chapter 14
Get Buffed or Bonk

In any given year, you can find a story or two of someone who got the sudden urge to hike and just hopped on trail and completed a very long thru-hike. You don't see the stories of the hundreds of others who got the same urge and failed because they were not prepared for a long hike. It's not difficult, but it is important to get in shape before taking on a long trail.

Tip #140 Prepare your legs by walking. The more miles you can walk every day, the better. If you only walk three miles every other Saturday, then start a long hike doing fifteen miles on the first day, it most likely won't work out well for you.

I'm fortunate to have time to walk about 5 or 6 miles most mornings and that means I'm able to hop on trail pretty much any time someone wants to go.

Tip #141 Prepare your feet by walking in the shoes and socks you'll use on trail. Wear them every day that you can, and walk as many miles in them as you have time. Many blisters can be prevented by having your feet used to your shoes.

I found a shoe that works very well for me. I have a couple new pairs of them still sitting in boxes at home, waiting for me to need them. This way, I won't have the hassle and stress of quickly figuring out what shoe to buy for my next hike when these are no longer available. I'll be able to take my time and find another shoe that's perfect for me while wearing out these extra pairs.

Tip #142   Prepare your body by carrying your pack. Just walking is fine, but the extra 20 pounds or more of your pack makes a big difference. By carrying your pack on your practice hikes, your shoulders and waist get used to it and you are better psychologically prepared as well.

Tip #143   Prepare for the expected terrain. If you live in flat land and will be doing a mountainous long hike, find ways to simulate ups and downs. Hike up and down the longest, steepest hills around. Use stairs instead of elevators. Hike the bleachers at the high school football field, or maybe a basketball court. Working your "Going Up" muscles is very important because they are different from your "Flat Walking" muscles.

Tip #144   Upper body muscle is extra weight. For a long-distance hiker, the feet, legs, heart, and lungs are key. Your core needs to be strong, but arm strength is not very important. Anyway, that's my excuse for being so skinny.

Chapter 15
Do or Die

Everyone knows the biggest danger on any trail is BEARS! Actually, your chances of being killed by a bear while hiking are about the same as getting killed by a shark. It very rarely happens. There are many other more common and easy ways to get injured or killed out in nature. If a prepared hiker avoids these, then they can spend more time worrying about bears.

Tip #145 Beware the Boardwalks – Falling is the most common method of injury and death for hikers. Unstable terrain, such as snow, scree, and gravel are dangerous, but with just a little rain, or even morning dew, boardwalks over permanently wet areas or fragile vegetation can be treacherous. Step directly, flatly, and slowly onto boardwalks to ensure you have traction.

Besides boardwalks, other smooth surfaces such as bedrock, logs, and even paved roads are more prone to being slippery. It only takes a little water, frost, or sand on the surface to make it treacherous.

I slipped three different times on my Superior Hiking Trail thru-hike – all from my first step onto a boardwalk being at a bit of an angle and hitting my heel first, losing traction, and doing a slow-motion splits with my front leg just refusing to stop. Unfortunately, on one slip, I landed on a hiking pole and broke it. No injuries, though. I was just hiking too fast and not paying attention as I should.

Tip #146 Beware the Selfie – Stay safe and respect nature when going for the perfect picture.

Maintain awareness of your footing and don't trample vegetation to get the best angle. "Just a bit farther" has killed a lot of photographer-wanna-bes.

Tip #147   Beware the Summit Fever – Pushing limits to reach a goal sometimes kills people. While forcing your way higher to reach a summit as the rain pours, lightning flashes, and wind blows, you should stop and consider the risks versus rewards. Evaluate each situation and know you can try some other time if it doesn't look doable this time. Mountains don't move, and neither do trails. You can come back and finish the hike another day.

I met a fellow long distance hiker named PapaBear two weeks into my thru hike of the Arizona Trail, and we hiked together for many days. One morning just north of Pine, AZ, we woke to about 6 inches of fresh snow. Rather than continuing our hike in dangerous conditions, we hitched a ride to town and waited a few days for the snow to melt.

Tip #148   Exposure – Excessively high or low levels of temperature and humidity can cause frostbite, hypothermia, heat stroke, or dehydration. Ensure you have   appropriate   clothing   and   skills   for   the temperature and weather extremes you will face on your hike.

Many nights on the Arizona Trail, the temperature would plummet as soon as the sun set because the dry air held little heat. One day was 90F degrees and I had frost in my tent the next morning. I was very glad I had brought a down jacket on my hike through the desert.

Tip #149   Beware the Currents – Fording a river, or even a small stream, is a dangerous undertaking. Drowning is a surprisingly common cause of death for long distance hikers. Shallow moving water, combined with slippery footing, can easily knock a person over and wash them downstream.

There are many ways to make water crossing safer. Use trekking poles for balance, and always keep three points of contact. Face upstream and shuffle sideways across, moving and placing one foot or pole at a time. Wear shoes rather than going barefoot. Cross at a wider, shallower location. Cross at a straight section where the riverbed tends to be flatter and shallower, rather than on a bend. Cross streams fed by melting snow in the early morning when water levels tend to be lower. Cross downstream from logs and branches in the water rather than above them.

Tip #150   Beware the Heartbeat – Medical problems take a heavy toll on hikers, especially men over 40 years old. The extra stress and strain of hiking all day over rough terrain is sometimes enough to trigger a heart attack. It can happen to anyone, but higher risks include: low fitness level, previous condition, overweight, high elevation, high temperature, hiking too fast.

It's a good idea to get a physical check before attempting a long hike. Tell your doctor what you are planning and find out what they think of your goals based on your current medical state.

An active exercise routine, healthy diet, healthy weight, and being tobacco-free are ways to help prevent heart problems. Once you are on the trail, limiting your miles and pace, staying hydrated and well-fed, and taking any prescribed medications can help prevent problems.

Bonus Appendix:
Say What?

Sometimes the words we have do not adequately describe a new thing, or are too inefficient for a conversation. Someone made up the word Google and it's now used as a company name, a verb, and a noun. Hiking is no different, and a hiking language exists and is constantly evolving. These are some of the more common words you might hear and use, but be aware that new ones show up every year.

10-by-10 – a daily goal of hiking 10 miles by 10am

Angel Food – food given to hikers by Trail Angels.

AYCE – All You Can Eat restaurant

Blaze – a marking that shows where a trail exists

Bear Bag – a lighter option to a Bear Can for protecting food.

Bear Bagging – the skill of properly hanging food when you have no Bear Can or Bear Bag.

Bear Burrito – when someone is asleep in a hammock or sleeping bag, they are a warm, soft, helpless snack for any bear happening by, hence the term.

Bear Can – a hard plastic canister to store food in as protection from animals.

Bear Pole – a tall metal pole with hooks from which food packs are hung.

Beaver Fever – giardia sickness from drinking untreated, contaminated water.

Big Three – the three items that tend to contribute the most weight to a hiker's pack – shelter, sleep system, and the pack itself.

Blowdown – a fallen tree blocking the trail.

Blowout – a shoe breaking or falling apart due to wear.

Boardwalk – wooden section of trail built over wet land.

Boink – running out of energy while hiking, also called Bonk. I skipped lunch and boinked hard before 2pm.

Bonus Miles – miles hiked off trail to a campsite, town, water source, etc. that do not count towards the length of the trail.

Bounce Box – important items that are not needed now but may be needed in the future. Items are mailed ahead to a post office farther down the trail to be picked up later.

Bubble – large group of hikers. Most long trail hikers tend to start within a short window of time that provides the best opportunity to finish, creating this moving group.

Bushwhacking – hiking off of an established trail.

Cairn – stack of rocks to mark a trail in an area where blazes are not practical or allowed, often rocky areas.

Cameling Up – drinking a lot at a water source so less water needs to be carried in containers.

Cat Hole – small hole dug in the ground as a make-shift toilet when it is needed and no toilet facilities are available.

Commando – not wearing underwear.

Cowboy Camp – sleeping with no tent or other shelter.

Cozy – insulation pack in which a container of food and hot water is placed to stay hot while the food rehydrates.

Death March – longer than normal day of hiking with little enjoyment.

Dirty Girls – low-cut, lightweight ankle gaiters

DIY – Do It Yourself, see MYOG.

Duff – soft forest floor covering of dead vegetation.

FKT – Fastest Known Time records the shortest time it has taken someone to hike an established trail.

FlipFlop – completing an entire long trail in one effort, but not from end-to-end. Due to weather, fire, or ease of terrain, someone might start in the middle and hike NoBo to the end, then hitch a ride back to the middle and hike SoBo to finish.

Floater – a bit of debris in water that can be picked out or removed by pouring the water through a bandanna.

Ford – walk through a river or stream to reach the other side.

Gear Head – a person consumed with researching equipment, and usually purchasing the very best of every possible item.

GORP – Good Old Raisins and Peanuts, old name for Trail Mix.

Gram Weenie – someone who is obsessed with reducing every conceivable bit of weight from their carried items.

Ground Control – a long distance hiker's support person at home who pays bills, sends mail drops, and the like.

Happy Camper – anyone who is feeling wonderful about their current situation.

Herd – mass of hikers heading the same direction, see Bubble.

Hermit Hiker – someone who does not interact with others on trail, at shelters, or other places where hikers mingle.

Hiker Box – place where hikers leave items they don't want and/or pick up items. Usually found at hostels or trail angel homes and tend to contain boring food or heavy gear.

Hiker Hobble – the way a hiker walks in the morning after days of hiking and they are stiff and sore.

Hiker Hunger – a constant feeling of hunger that is difficult to sate. It tends to occur after a couple weeks of hiking.

Hiker Midnight – time when everyone in a communal campsite or shelter is expected to be quiet so hikers can sleep. This is typically 9pm.

Hiker Tan –dust sticks to sweaty legs making them look dark and tanned, but only down to the sock or shoe line. When the legs are washed, the hiker tan is lost.

Hiker Trash – an endearing self-description that hikers

use. If a non-hiker were to use the term, it might cause trouble.

Hiker Widow(er) – a spouse at home who did not come on the hike and is forced to wait for the hiker to return.

Hostel – sleeping facility for travelers, typically with bunkroom style beds, showers, and food preparation areas.

HYOH – Hike Your Own Hike, traditionally meaning to hike in whatever way gives the most enjoyment as long as it does not impact other hikers negatively.

LASH – Long Ass Section Hike – a section hike that consumes a significant portion of a long trail. Someone attempting a thru-hike who stops part way through did a LASH.

LNT – Leave No Trace organization has developed seven principles to guide our recreational use of outdoors areas.

Loft – the amount of fluffiness of insulating gear.

MacGyver – fix something using whatever resources are available. I MacGyvered my blown out shoe with duct tape.

Mail Drop – a package of food mailed to a post office, hostel, or other facility that will hold it for a hiker to arrive.

Mooch – hiker who asks for food or assistance from other hikers rather than being prepared themselves.

Mountain Money – toilet paper

MYOG – Make Your Own Gear is a way to reduce the cost and increase the customization of equipment.

Nero Day – Nearly a Zero Day.

NoBo, SoBo, WeBo, EaBo – thru-hikers typically refer to themselves as: NOrthBOund hiker, SOuthBOund hiker, WOstBOund hiker, or EAstBOund hiker So, a SoBo on the PCT would run into a lot of NoBos, but a WeBo on the PNT might only meet 1 or 2 EaBos.

PUD – Pointless Ups and Downs – description of a section of trail that goes up and down hills with no perceived value, such as a great view at the top or waterfall along the way.

Puffy – a lightweight down jacket.

Purist – hiker who stringently adheres to the belief that every step of a trail must be traveled in order to claim a thru-hike.

Relo – a section of trail that has been relocated for some reason and may not be on current maps.

Resupply – replenishing food in a town for the next few days of trail until the next resupply.

Ride Bride – female hiker used by a male hiker to help get a ride when hitchhiking. Drivers may stop for a man and woman but not just a man. Some female hikers feel safer taking a ride when they have a male hiker with them.

Section Hike – hiking a portion of a long trail. By hiking in sections, an entire trail can be eventually hiked.

Shuttle – a ride to or from a town or any location off trail.

Skipping – leaving the trail to get a ride past some portion of trail, because of closure, difficulty, weather, or any reason.

Slackpack – hiking without a pack. A hiker might stay overnight with a trail angel who shuttles their pack a day's hike up the trail while they slackpack for the day.

Slog – monotonous hike through uninspiring areas, typically through mud, long uphills, or dreary weather.

Snake Stick – a stick that startles you as you hike past because it looks so much like a snake.

SoBo – see NoBo

Stealth Camp – camping in a manner to hide your presence because camping is not allowed. Dispersed or Wild camping is doing the same thing, but where camping is allowed.

Stick Snake – a snake that you thought was a stick after seeing so many snake sticks.

Switchback – the routing of a hiking trail up an incline so the trail goes back and forth across the slope rather than straight up the face. This causes the trail to be longer but less steep.

Tattoo – a wound scar acquired on a hike.

Thru-hike – hiking an entire trail in one hiking season. Typically, it is done in one go, from end to end, but that is not required.

Trail Angel – someone who provides trail magic

Trail Legs – conditioned legs that are able to hike long

distances, day after day.

Trail Magic – an unexpected event that happens on trail and inspires awe or gratitude. Could be finding a spoon just after losing yours, seeing a bear cub, being invited to a family's picnic, or getting a ride to town to resupply, for example.

Trail Name – a nickname taken by a hiker while on trail. It's common to never learn a fellow hiker's real name and only call them by their trail name for weeks.

Trail Spice – dirt, when it gets on your food.

Tramily – a group of hikers you meet on trail and hike with. Short for 'Trail Family'.

Triple Crown – In the USA, completing the Appalachian Trail, Continental Divide Trail, and Pacific Crest Trail.

Vitamin I – ibuprofen

Vortex – a trail town can suck a hiker off the trail and they can get stuck in the vortex for days, enjoying the comforts, instead of hiking.

Water Cache – water left for hikers in dry sections. Typically many 1 gallon plastic jugs stocked by trail angels.

Widow Maker – a dead branch or tree that could fall on your tent at night.

YMMV – Your Mileage May Vary. Something that works for me may not work as well for you (or work better).

Yogi – to inconspicuously convince someone to help you, similar to mooching but without asking directly. Something like, "Wow, what kind of candy bar is that?" with the hopes they will share it with you.

YoYo – hiking a trail from one end to the other and then turning around and hiking it back to the origin.

Zero Day – a day without hiking any trail miles, typically in a town to resupply, wash clothes, sleep in a bed, and recover.

About The Author

Paul Kautz hikes, writes, cooks, and teaches others. After many years of backpacking, leading Boy Scout trips, and doing short hikes, he found his passion for long-distance hiking after turning 50 years old.

When his two sons earned their Eagle Scout awards and he passed the troop he was the scoutmaster for on to another volunteer, his resulting free time needed to be filled. So, he did his first thru-hike in 2012, of the 800-mile Arizona Trail. This has been followed up by the Superior Hiking Trail, Ice Age Trail, Pacific Northwest Trail, West Coast Trail, Kekekabic Trail, Border Route Trail, and, most recently, Camino de Costa Rica. He has hiked hundreds of miles on the Florida Trail and Appalachian Trail, choosing to do section hikes rather than thru-hikes on them. He typically hikes about two thousand miles a year, between local hiking and long trails.

Paul embraces technology in the outdoors as long as it doesn't adversely impact the recreation of others. He loves to blog from the trail so others can get a sense of what hiking is like in real time. You can read all about his long hikes and adventures on HikingDude.com

Paul lives in Eden Prairie, MN with his patient wife.

Hike On!